The Little Book of God's Love

THE LITTLE BOOK OF
GOD'S
LOVE

Compiled by Philip Law

A LION BOOK

This edition copyright © 1999 Lion Publishing

Published by
Lion Publishing plc
Sandy Lane West, Oxford, England
www.lion-publishing.co.uk
ISBN 0 7459 4074 9

First edition 1999
10 9 8 7 6 5 4 3 2 1 0

All rights reserved

A catalogue record for this book is available from the British Library

Printed and bound in Great Britain by Caledonian International Book Manufacturing, Glasgow

GOD IS LOVE.
WHOEVER LIVES IN LOVE LIVES IN GOD,
AND GOD IN HIM.

ST JOHN (1 JOHN 4:16)

To say that God is love is to say that God is the living, active, dynamic, ceaselessly desiring reality who will not let go until he has won the free response of his creation.

NORMAN PITTENGER

Love unites the soul with God, and, the more degrees of love the soul has, the more profoundly does it enter into God and the more is it centred in him.

St John of the Cross

Contemplation is nothing else but a secret, peaceful and loving infusion of God, which, if admitted, will set the soul on fire with the spirit of love.

ST JOHN OF THE CROSS

He who is filled with love
is filled with God himself.

St Augustine of Hippo

'You shall love the Lord your God with all your heart, and with all your soul, and with all your mind.' This is the greatest and first commandment. And a second is like it: 'You shall love your neighbour as yourself.'

JESUS (MATTHEW 22:37–39)

He alone loves the Creator perfectly who manifests a pure love for his neighbour.

The Venerable Bede

Love for our neighbour consists of three things:
to desire the greater good of everyone;
to do what good we can when we can;
to bear, excuse and hide others' faults.

ST JEAN VIANNEY

*Love seeketh not itself to please,
nor for itself hath any care,
but for another gives its ease,
and builds a heaven in hell's despair.*

WILLIAM BLAKE

Love seeks only one thing:
the good of the one loved.
It leaves all the other secondary
effects to take care of themselves.

Thomas Merton

Love is self-sufficient: it is pleasing to itself and on its own account. Love is its own payment, its own reward.

St Bernard of Clairvaux

Love is strong as death...
Many waters cannot quench love,
neither can floods drown it.

SONG OF SOLOMON 8:6, 7

A soul cannot live without loving. It must have something to love, for it was created to love.

ST CATHERINE OF SIENA

Love needs to be made
like good bread, newly each day,
to keep its freshness.

Michaela Davis

Only love enables humanity to grow, because love engenders life and it is the only form of energy that lasts for ever.

MICHEL QUOIST

To grow is to emerge gradually from a land where our vision is limited, where we are seeking and governed by egotistical pleasure, by our sympathies and antipathies, to a land of unlimited horizons and universal love, where we will be open to every person and desire their happiness.

JEAN VANIER

We were born to love, we live to love, and we will die to love still more.

JOSEPH CAFASSO

Though I have the gift of prophecy,
and understand all mysteries,
and all knowledge;
and though I have all faith,
so that I could remove mountains,
and have not love, I am nothing.

St Paul (I Corinthians 13:2)

When we say: 'Yes, I doubt, but I do believe in God's love more than I trust my own doubts,' it becomes possible for God to act.

ANTHONY BLOOM

GOD CAN DO EVERYTHING,
EXCEPT COMPEL A MAN TO LOVE HIM.

PAUL EVDOKIMOV

God will always answer our prayers; but he will answer them in his way, and his way will be the way of perfect wisdom and of perfect love. Often if he answered our prayers as we at the moment desire, it would be the worst thing possible for us, for in our ignorance we often ask for gifts which would be our ruin.

WILLIAM BARCLAY

God did not say, 'You shall not be tempest-tossed, you shall not be work-weary, you shall not be discomforted.' But he said, 'You shall not be overcome.'

JULIAN OF NORWICH

Trust the past to God's mercy,
the present to God's love and
the future to God's providence.

St Augustine of Hippo

God has never been seen by anyone, but if we love one another, he himself dwells in us; his love is brought to perfection within us.

St John (1 John 4:12)

In this world is God. Man is able to see God, not in the intellectual process, but in the feeling of value, whose purest form is love. There is a genuine recognition of value only in love. In love man soars to the vision of the eternal and highest value of the holy.

Dietrich Bonhoeffer

A saint is a human creature devoured and transformed by love: a love that has dissolved and burnt out those instinctive passions – acquisitive and combative, proud and greedy – which commonly rule the lives of men.

EVELYN UNDERHILL

Love is infallible;
it has no errors,
for all errors are
the want of love.

WILLIAM LAW

Let brotherly love continue. Be not forgetful to entertain strangers: for thereby some have entertained angels unawares.

ANONYMOUS (HEBREWS 13:1–2)

Remember that the ones
you love in your heart are
but guests in your soul.

Jim Cotter

*A joyful heart is the normal result
of a heart burning with love.*

MOTHER TERESA OF CALCUTTA

> YOU CAN GIVE WITHOUT LOVING,
> BUT YOU CANNOT LOVE WITHOUT GIVING.
>
> AMY CARMICHAEL

LIVING IN OUR SELFISHNESS MEANS STOPPING AT HUMAN LIMITS AND PREVENTING OUR TRANSFORMATION INTO DIVINE LOVE.

CARLO CARRETTO

To love is to be willing to put the beloved in the first place and oneself in the second place.

NORMAN PITTENGER

There is no fear in love. But perfect love drives out fear, because fear has to do with punishment. The one who fears is not made perfect in love.

St John (1 John 4:18)

The first step in personhood is to allow ourselves to be loved. To know ourselves loved is to have the depths of our own capacity to love opened up.

JOHN MAIN

Since God loves you anyway,
there is no point in making yourself out
to be better than you are – and none in
making yourself out to be worse.

WILLIAM COUNTRYMAN

THE PERSON YOU ARE NOW,
THE PERSON YOU HAVE BEEN,
THE PERSON YOU WILL YET BE —
THIS PERSON GOD HAS CHOSEN AS BELOVED.

WILLIAM COUNTRYMAN

*God loves you as though you are
the only person in the world, and he
loves everyone the way he loves you.*

St Augustine of Hippo

Love your enemies; do good to those who hate you... If you love only those who love you, what credit is that to you? Even sinners love those who love them.

JESUS (LUKE 6:27, 32)

NOTHING ELSE CAN WITHSTAND EVIL
EXCEPT THE POWER OF LOVE.

UNA KROLL

Love is the only force capable of transforming an enemy into a friend.

MARTIN LUTHER KING

*Where there is no love, pour love in,
and you will draw love out.*

ST JOHN OF THE CROSS

THE FIRST DUTY OF LOVE IS TO LISTEN.

PAUL TILLICH

Most people have the best of intentions,
but they are not secure enough
to express love by listening in depth
when others express some idea
or intention that they believe is wrong.

MORTON T. KELSEY

LOVE'S FINEST SPEECH IS WITHOUT WORDS.

HADEWIJCH OF BRABANT

At the heart of every human being is the ear of God. Human ears hear human voices. God's ear hears the voice of the heart.

St Augustine of Hippo

As God's chosen ones, holy and beloved, clothe yourselves with compassion, kindness, humility, meekness and patience. Bear with one another and, if anyone has a complaint against another, forgive each other... Above all, clothe yourselves with love, which binds everything together in perfect harmony.

ST PAUL (COLOSSIANS 3:12–14)

We must develop and maintain the capacity to forgive. He who is devoid of the power to forgive is devoid of the power to love.

MARTIN LUTHER KING

We pardon as long as we love.

FRANÇOIS, DUC DE LA ROCHEFOUCAULD

Be kind and merciful. Let no one ever come to you without coming away better and happier. Be the living expression of God's kindness: kindness in your face, kindness in your eyes, kindness in your smile, kindness in your warm greeting.

MOTHER TERESA OF CALCUTTA

Love is patient; love is kind; love is not envious or boastful or arrogant or rude. It does not insist on its own way; it is not irritable or resentful; it does not rejoice in wrongdoing, but rejoices in the truth. It bears all things, believes all things, hopes all things, endures all things. Love never ends.

St Paul (I Corinthians 13:4–8)

It is good to love many things, for therein lies strength. Whosoever loves much can accomplish much, and what is done with love is well done.

VINCENT VAN GOGH

For those who love, nothing is hard;
and no task is difficult if your desire is great.

ST JEROME

THE WHOLE OF HUMAN LIFE IS BUT A SINGLE DAY,
TO THOSE WHO LABOUR WITH LOVE.

ST GREGORY OF NAZIANZUS

The paths of love are both long and short...
abounding both in fresh thoughts and in old
memories.

RAYMOND LULL

Leave all your worries with God,
because he cares for you.

St Peter (1 Peter 5:7)

Love for God is ecstatic, making us go out from ourselves.

DIONYSIUS THE AREOPAGITE

By love he may be gotten and holden,
but by thought never.

The Cloud of Unknowing

Don't try to reach God with your understanding; that is impossible. Reach him in love; that is possible.

CARLO CARRETTO

By love alone is God enjoyed, by love alone delighted in, by love alone approached and admired. His nature requires love.

THOMAS TRAHERNE

Love, by its nature, is a resemblance to God, insofar as this is humanly possible... Its distinctive character is to be a fountain of faith, an abyss of patience, a sea of humility.

ST JOHN CLIMACUS

Let all that you do be done in love.

St Paul (I Corinthians 16:14)

God makes of *all* things mysteries and sacraments of love; why should not every moment of our lives be a sort of communion with the divine love?

JEAN PIERRE DE CAUSSADE

It is only by fidelity in little things that a true and constant love of God can be distinguished from a passing fervour of spirit.

FRANÇOIS FÉNELON

To worship is to quicken the conscience by the holiness of God, to feed the mind with the truth of God, to purge the imagination by the beauty of God, to open the heart to the love of God, to devote the will to the purpose of God.

WILLIAM TEMPLE

Love one another, just as I love you.

Jesus (John 15:12)

What makes the temptation of power so seemingly irresistible? Maybe it is that power offers an easy substitute for the hard task of love. It seems easier to be God than to love God, easier to control people than to love people, easier to own life than to love life.

HENRI NOUWEN

The act of love – extending oneself – requires a moving out against the inertia of laziness (work) or the resistance engendered by fear (courage)… When we extend ourselves, our self enters new and unfamiliar territory, so to speak. Our self becomes a new and different self. We do things we are not accustomed to do. We change.

M. Scott Peck

MYSTICISM IS THE NAME OF THAT ORGANIC
PROCESS WHICH INVOLVES THE PERFECT
CONSUMMATION OF THE LOVE OF GOD.

EVELYN UNDERHILL

Above all, maintain constant love for one another, for love covers a multitude of sins.

St Peter (I Peter 4:8)

*Sin is always loving badly,
or not loving at all.*

MICHEL QUOIST

VIRTUE IS NOTHING BUT
WELL-DIRECTED LOVE.

ST AUGUSTINE OF HIPPO

Grace is love that cares
and stoops and rescues.

John Stott

He who loves not his
brother abides in death.

St John (1 John 3:14)

*No matter how deep
our darkness,
he is deeper still.*

CORRIE TEN BOOM

*You never lose the love of God.
Guilt is the warning that
temporarily you are out of touch.*

JACK DOMINIAN

It is only when we have lost all love of ourselves for our own sakes, that our past sins cease to give us the anguish of shame.

THOMAS MERTON

If a man say, I love God,
and hates his brother, he is a liar:
for whoever does not love his brother,
whom he has seen, how can he love God,
whom he has not seen?

St John (I John 4:20)

He does not believe who does not love according to his beliefs.

Thomas Fuller

Truth and love are wings that cannot be separated, for truth cannot fly without love, nor can love soar aloft without truth.

ST EPHRAEM THE SYRIAN

*Truth sees God: wisdom gazes on God.
And these two produce a third, a holy,
wondering delight in God, which is love.*

JULIAN OF NORWICH

If anyone has the world's goods and sees his brother in need, yet closes his heart against him, how does God's love abide in him?

St John (1 John 3:17)

It is only inasmuch as you see someone as he or she really is here and now, and not as they are in your memory or your desire or in your imagination or projection, that you can truly love them.

ANTHONY DE MELLO

The best portion of a good man's life,
his little, nameless, unremembered acts
of kindness and of love…

WILLIAM WORDSWORTH

To ears which have been trained to wait upon God in silence, and in the quietness of meditation and prayer, a very small incident, or a word, may prove to be a turning point in our lives, and a new opening for his love to enter our world, to create and to redeem.

OLIVE WYON

Greater love has no man than this, that a man lay down his life for his friends.

JESUS (JOHN 15:13)

Were the whole realm of nature mine,
That were an offering far too small:
Love so amazing, so divine
Demands my soul, my life, my all.

Isaac Watts

To be able to say how much love,
is to love but little.

FRANCESCO PETRARCH

Only love lasts for ever. Alone, it constructs the shape of eternity in the earthly and short-lived dimensions of the history of man on the earth.

POPE JOHN PAUL II

'Behold, the dwelling of God is with men... He will wipe away every tear from their eyes, and death shall be no more, neither shall there be mourning nor crying nor pain any more, for the former things have passed away.'

St John (Revelation 21:3, 4)

Acknowledgments
We would like to thank all those who have given us permission to include material in this book. Every effort has been made to trace and acknowledge copyright holders of all the quotations in this book. We apologize for any errors or omissions that may remain, and would ask those concerned to contact the publishers, who will ensure that full acknowledgment is made in the future.

Extracts on pages 5 and 38 are taken from the *Holy Bible, New International Version*, copyright © 1973, 1978, 1984 by International Bible Society. Used by permission.

Extracts on pages 10, 16, 51, 55, 66 and 74 are taken from The New Revised Standard Version of the Bible, Anglicized Edition, copyright © 1989, 1995 by the Division of Christian Education of the National Council of the Churches of Christ in the United States of America, and are used by permission. All rights reserved.

Extracts on pages 22, 32, 78 and 82 are taken from the Authorized Version of the Bible (The King James Bible), the rights in which are vested in the Crown, and are reproduced by permission of the Crown's Patentee, Cambridge University Press.

Extracts on pages 28 and 43 are taken from the Revised English Bible © 1989 by permission of Oxford and Cambridge University Presses.

Extracts on pages 60 and 70 are taken from the Good News Bible, published by the Bible Societies/HarperCollins Publishers Ltd, UK © American Bible Society 1966, 1971, 1976, 1992, used with permission.

Extracts on pages 86, 90 and 94 are taken from The Revised Standard Version of the Bible, copyright © 1946, 1952, 1971 by the Division of Christian Education of the National Council of the Churches of Christ in the United States of America, and are used by permission. All rights reserved.